Festival Te Deum

founded on traditional themes

R. VAUGHAN WILLIAMS

All ___ the earth doth wor-ship thee: the_ Fa - ther ev - er - last -

- ing.

To thee all An - gels cry___ a - loud: the

OXFORD CHURCH SERVICES

neral Editor David Willcocks

177

A.T.B.

Festival Te Deum

founded on traditional themes

by

R. Vaughan Williams

Music Department
OXFORD UNIVERSITY PRESS
Oxford and New York

Full Score and Orchestral Parts
may be hired

The good-ly fel-low-ship of the Pro-phets: praise ___ thee; ___

The no - ble ar- my of Mar - tyrs: praise ___

___ thee; ___ The ho - ly Church through -

ISBN 978-0-19-351530-7